TIME FOR KIDS READERS

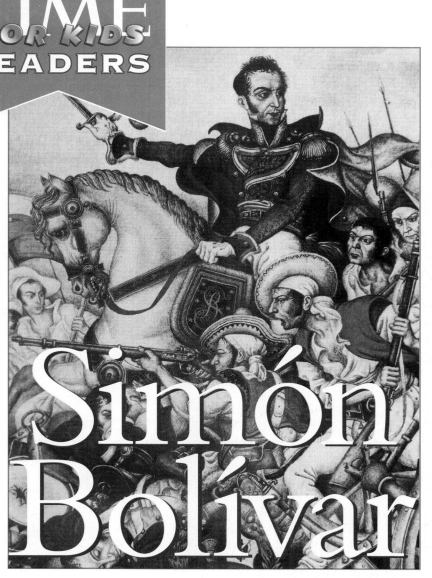

Simón Bolívar

by Roberta Ann Cruise

Harcourt

Orlando   Austin   Chicago   New York   Toronto   London   San Diego

Visit *The Learning Site!*
www.harcourtschool.com

Father of Many Countries

People in the United States and around the world know about George Washington. He was our first president, the "father of our country." He helped shape our young nation as it was being formed, leaving his mark on our history and our government.

Simón Bolívar (see•MOHN boh•LEE•var) is often called the George Washington of South America, as well as South America's Liberator. Bolívar was born in Venezuela. Like Washington, he was a leader of his country's fight for independence. He also led the fight for independence all across South America. In Venezuela, Colombia, Ecuador, and Peru, he fought against Spanish rule. Washington had a city and a state named after him. Bolívar had Bolivia, an entire country, named after him.

How did one man affect the history of so many nations? He was the right man at the right moment. He lived at a time when countries across South America were crying out for independence. Also, he was a very remarkable man.

Small Boy, Big Name

Simón Bolívar was not his full name. Simón José Antonio de la Santísima Trinidad de Bolívar y Palacios was born on July 24, 1783—the last year of the American Revolution—in Caracas, Venezuela.

Bolívar's ancestors had left Spain to settle in South America in 1548. They had become very rich in the Americas. They had a large house in Caracas and a big country home nearby at San Mateo.

The Bolívar household was big and busy. Simón had an older brother and two older sisters. His parents were important people in Venezuela. The Bolívars owned silver and copper mines, cattle ranches, and plantations throughout Venezuela. The family's huge plantations raised cacao, sugar-cane, and other valuable crops.

Simón's mother was stern and sometimes too busy to pay much attention to the Bolívar children. His father was often away from the family. He died when Simón was three years old.

To Bolívar's ancestors, this is how the Americas appeared on a map.

Young Bolívar, who had dark eyes and dark, curly hair, was known for his bold spirit. He especially liked to ride horses. Yet, because he was small for his age, he had to start out riding a burro. Bolívar was eager to race a real horse around his family's country estate!

The world that Simón Bolívar was born into had strong class divisions. The Bolívars were part of the upper class. They were rich and used enslaved people to do all their work. The Bolívars were much better off than the Native American tribes and free Africans who lived in Venezuela. Still, the Bolívars and people like them were ruled by yet another class of people.

The really powerful people were the colonial rulers sent by the king of Spain. Even rich people like the Bolívars had to treat them with special respect. The Bolívars and others like them were forced to pay high taxes but

The Bolívar family owned a great deal of land in the Venezuelan countryside.

4

had little say about what happened in the colony. The Spanish governors kept a close eye on colonial landowners like the Bolívars. The governors even decided what books the colonials were allowed to read. Simón Bolívar grew up with a keen understanding of the importance of freedom.

When Simón was nine years old, he began his lifelong lessons in freedom. His mother died, and he went to live with his uncle, Carlos. However, it was an enslaved woman named Hipólita and her helper, Matea, who really raised him. Hipólita had worked for the family for many years. She was kind and loving toward young Simón. Near the end of his life, Bolívar wrote fondly of Hipólita, "I know no other parent but her." From her he had learned about the injustice of slavery. Helping end slavery would become an important part of Bolívar's long fight for freedom.

In parts of South America, slaves grew sugarcane on plantations.

A World of Ideas

When Simón was a boy, he had a long parade of private tutors, including a poet, a priest, and a German scientist. One tutor described his energetic student as "a keg of dynamite." Simón told the tutor to stay away from him. "I might explode," the boy warned.

As a boy, Simón loved to read. He especially loved the book *Don Quixote* (DOHN kee•HOH•tay). It tells of the adventures of a Spanish knight with a strong imagination. The brave knight is hopeful. He believes that goodness and right will always win over evil and might. *Don Quixote* made an impression on Simón. Throughout his life, he read the book again and again—even during the last few days before his death.

Simón Bolívar became more serious about learning after the death of both his parents. His uncle arranged for a young man named Simón Rodríguez to take charge of the boy. The new tutor played an important role in Bolívar's life. Rodríguez taught Simón to question the way society was run. At the time, around 1790, new ideas about freedom and democracy were being discussed everywhere. The American Revolution had been followed by the French Revolution. Many people were thinking and writing about placing power in the hands of ordinary people and taking it away from royal rulers.

The story character Don Quixote (near right) and his down-to-earth sidekick, Sancho Panza (far right).

Rodríguez taught his student about philosophers and their ideas. One philosopher they studied was Jean-Jacques Rousseau (zhahn•ZHAHK roo•SOH). He was a French philosopher who wrote that all people are born free and equal. He also believed that people should live close to nature.

Rodríguez made young Simón test Rousseau's ideas about nature. Teacher and student moved from Caracas to the Bolívars' country home at San Mateo. For five years they hiked and swam and rode horses. Simón's mind grew sharper as he studied harder. Rodríguez was proud of his eager young student.

Jean-Jacques Rousseau
1712–1778

A Teenager in Europe

Rodríguez left for Europe when Simón was 14 years old. It was at this time that Simón decided to become a cadet in a military unit that his father had organized. Simón was an expert with a sword and was also skilled at horseback riding. However, his relatives decided that being in the military was not a good life for the teenager. The relatives arranged for Simón to study in Spain. He was 15 years old when he set sail for Europe in January 1799. While stopping in Mexico on the way to Madrid, he spoke out boldly for freedom, equality, and revolution. Simón Bolívar had not forgotten the important lessons that Rodríguez had taught him.

Simón arrived in Madrid in the spring of 1799. In November of that year, Napoleon Bonaparte, a powerful French military leader, became the ruler of France. Napoleon was a military dictator, but he spoke about the ideals of the French Revolution, including liberty and equality. For that reason, many people admired Napoleon. What an exciting time to be in Europe! The talk everywhere was about freedom.

Simón Bolívar was still a teenager. Fancy parties interested him a lot more than European politics. Still, it didn't hurt that he quickly made friends with some of the most important—and wealthiest—people in Madrid. He even met the king of Spain, Charles IV, and queen and came to know their oldest son, Prince Ferdinand.

One summer day in 1799, Prince Ferdinand and Simón Bolívar were matched against each other in a game of racquetball. When Simón accidentally knocked Ferdinand's hat off his head, the young prince became angry. Ferdinand demanded an apology. Bolívar refused to say he was sorry. Queen María Luisa made peace between the two stubborn young men, and they resumed their game.

Little did they know that 20 years later they would cross paths again. Ferdinand would then be the king of Spain. Bolívar would lead South America's fight for independence. Recalling the incident, Bolívar said, "Who would have prophesied to Ferdinand . . . that this was a sign that one day I might tear the costliest jewel from his crown?"

When he was 17 years old, Simón fell in love with a wealthy young woman, María Teresa de Toro. Her parents approved of him. Like Simón, María had been born in the colonies, not in Spain. However, they believed that the 17-year-old and their daughter were too young to marry. They made a suggestion—Bolívar would spend one year exploring

Europe. He and María Teresa would be permitted to marry if and when he returned to Madrid. Bolívar agreed, and in 1801 he left for Paris.

Simón enjoyed the hustle and bustle of life in Paris. He had the time and the money to live well. However, he was eager to find his way back to María Teresa de Toro. At last their year apart ended. Bolívar and de Toro were married in May 1802.

The young couple set sail for Venezuela and soon settled into one of the Bolívars' big homes. They lived happily together, but not for long. In January 1803, María Teresa suddenly became ill and died. Her death was a turning point for Bolívar. Not even 21 years old, he swore that he would never remarry. He told a friend, "If I had not lost her, I would not have been General Bolívar or the Liberator."

Francisco José de Goya y Lucientes painted this portrait of the family of Charles IV around 1800.

An Idea Takes Hold

Bolívar was too sad to stay in Venezuela. In 1804 he returned to Madrid. There, too, memories of María Teresa filled him with sorrow. Bolívar once again headed for France, where he became more interested in politics.

Napoleon still ruled France. He had crowned himself emperor and had set out to conquer much of Europe. He was still popular in France, but many people were beginning to believe that he was little more than a dictator. Bolívar wrote in a letter, "I admire his gifts as a soldier, but can't you see that he is simply aiming at personal power? The man is becoming a tyrant."

Bolívar was also becoming unhappy with the king and queen of Spain. Like many other people, he thought Charles was a weak and unfair king. Now Bolívar began to pay more attention to talk of democracy and independence. He began to wonder if it was time for Venezuela to break free from Spain.

At about this time, Bolívar met up with his former tutor, Simón Rodríguez. The two traveled together, exploring Europe from France to Italy. Bolívar was especially excited to be in Rome and was influenced by stories of the ancient Romans. Bolívar spent three years in Europe on this trip. By the time the trip was over, he had made some important decisions.

In 1806 a man named Francisco de Miranda tried to start a war of independence in Venezuela. He failed, but that attempt inspired Bolívar. In early 1807 he decided to return to Venezuela and join the fight against Spain.

Just a year later the French emperor invaded Spain and forced King Charles to give up the throne. Napoleon made his own brother, Joseph, the new ruler of Spain. Some Spanish people welcomed Joseph. Others wanted the prince, Ferdinand, to become king. Britain, which was at war with Napoleon, supported Ferdinand. The British invaded Spain to drive out Napoleon.

Napoleon changed the course of South American history and the life of Simón Bolívar. The people in Spain's colonies had to choose. Should they be loyal

The *Consecration of Napoleon and the Coronation Of Empress Josephine (December 2, 1804)* was painted by French artist Jacques-Louis David.

to Ferdinand, the son of their former king? Or should they side with Napoleon and the new ruler of Spain? While war raged in Spain, many South Americans decided the time was right to fight for independence. Simón Bolívar was among them.

On with the Fight!

In Venezuela, Bolívar started a secret group called the Patriotic Society. Its goal was independence for all of Spain's colonies in the Americas. In Caracas, on April 19, 1810, a group of rebels demanded to talk to the new Venezuelan governor. The governor asked the people who had gathered in the streets if they wanted him to continue as their governor. The answer was a bold "No!" Without a gun being fired, Venezuela proclaimed its freedom.

The rebels set up a representative government based on the government of the United States. Other Spanish colonies, including Argentina, Colombia, Chile, and Ecuador, followed this example. But Spain would not let its colonies go without a fight. Even while the Spanish and the British were fighting Napoleon, Prince Ferdinand was getting ready to send the Spanish army to take control of his colonies.

In Venezuela, Bolívar joined with Francisco de Miranda to build an army. On July 5, 1811, Venezuela became the first Spanish colony in South America to officially proclaim its freedom. Spain's response was fast and furious. Ferdinand sent troops to regain control. The rebel army was not as well trained or organized. By July 1812 the Spanish troops were once more in charge.

Miranda was arrested and jailed, but the new governor didn't realize that Bolívar had also been a leader of the rebellion. The governor allowed Bolívar to leave Venezuela.

The rebel had been forced to give up most of his possessions. He would never again be wealthy. That didn't matter to Bolívar. He had found his mission in life. He would continue to lead the rebel troops in the fight for independence. Bolívar hoped that one day all of the countries in South America would be free. He also hoped that those countries would form a united republic, like the United States of America.

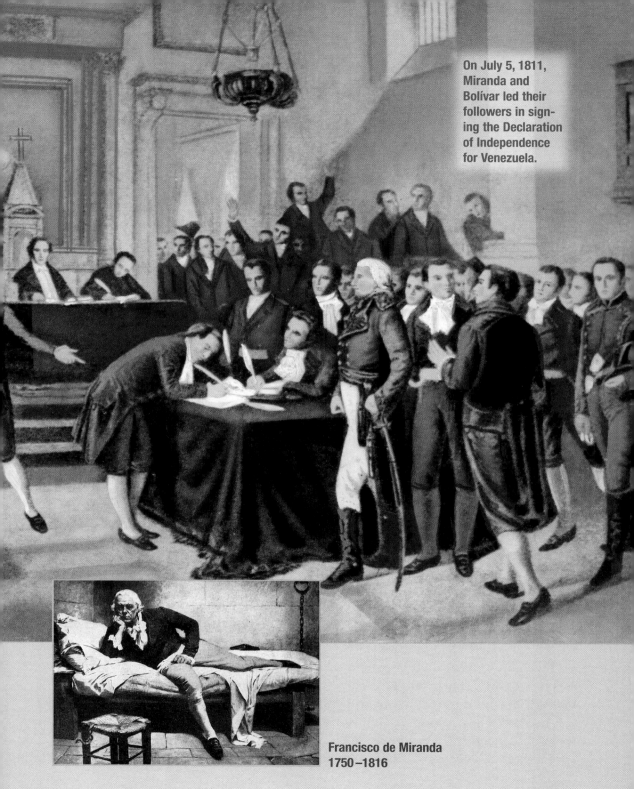

On July 5, 1811, Miranda and Bolívar led their followers in signing the Declaration of Independence for Venezuela.

Francisco de Miranda
1750–1816

The Liberator

Almost at once, Bolívar started raising a new army. His goal was to take control of Caracas and the rest of Venezuela. He thought this would lead to independence for Colombia and for other Spanish colonies as well. The war that followed was brutal.

Even nature seemed to be fighting against the rebels. A major earthquake killed thousands of rebel soldiers in Caracas on March 26, 1812. However, most of the Spanish soldiers in the city were not hurt. Many people believed the earthquake was a sign that Spain had God on its side. Despite the disaster, Bolívar was not about to give up. "Even if Nature itself opposes us, we will not give in," Bolívar said. "We will [fight] Nature too, and force it to obey us!"

Bolívar and the rebel troops were more determined than ever to defeat Spain. The revolution was called the "War to the Death." Both the rebels and the Spanish killed many innocent people. The rebels vowed to kill or imprison any colonists who remained loyal to Spain. Slowly, the rebels made their way toward the capital city of Caracas.

The Caracas earthquake of 1812 destroyed Bolívar's home.

Each time Bolívar and his troops freed a town, he would send out a message. In his message he wrote *libertada* (liberated) after the name of every town the rebels freed. On August 6, 1813, Bolívar led his army into Caracas. The city was free once again. Crowds celebrated with fireworks and dancing in the streets. The people cheered Bolívar as El Libertador, the Liberator who had freed Venezuela.

Freedom for Venezuela lasted less than a year. Napoleon had been driven from Spain and Ferdinand had become king in March 1814. Ferdinand was determined to control the colonies, and he sent more and more troops to South America. By June 1814 Spain once again ruled Venezuela. The revolution had failed for a second time. Once more Bolívar fled Venezuela.

14

Joseph Bonaparte was the king of Spain from 1808 to 1814.

Victory and Independence

In June 1815 Bolívar landed on the British-held Caribbean island of Jamaica. While there he wrote an essay that came to be known as the Jamaica Letter. In the essay Bolívar explained his plan for a union that would include all South American nations. "A people that loves freedom in the end will be free," he wrote. He was more determined than ever to see South America become the "greatest nation in the world."

Bolívar was also determined to be the person who would make that happen. In 1816 he once again set out for Venezuela. This time he had the support of the country of Haiti, a small republic in the West Indies. Haiti had been a French colony until the enslaved Africans there rose up in rebellion and took control of the country. Now the former slaves in Haiti wanted to end slavery everywhere. In return for their support, Bolívar promised to help end slavery in South America. He landed in Venezuela and raised another army. Once more he marched toward Caracas.

This time Bolívar worked harder to make sure the rebellion wouldn't fail. In each town they liberated, the rebels set up a new government to take the place of the Spanish rulers. In February 1819 Bolívar's troops reached the small Venezuelan town of Angostura (ahn•go•STOO•rah), which is now called Bolívar City. There, Bolívar said the time had come for the entire country to have a new government. Bolívar was elected president of the new republic.

During his stay in Angostura, Bolívar came up with a new, daring plan. He announced it at a fancy dinner. Dressed in his best uniform, Bolívar climbed onto a table to announce that he was going to lead his troops to free Colombia. To do this, they would have to march over the Andes Mountains and across hundreds of miles of difficult ground.

Bolívar and his men crossed the Andes, one of the highest mountain ranges in the world. **17**

While a rebel army remained to fight in Venezuela, Bolívar led another force toward Colombia. They set out on February 27, 1819. They slogged through raging rivers and swamps teeming with alligators. They staggered through heavy rain and climbed 12,000-foot (3,658-m) snowcapped mountains. All of their horses died or went lame along the way. Hundreds of soldiers starved or froze to death.

Slowly but steadily, Bolívar and his army marched forward. The troops were tired but determined. They won battle after battle, and on August 7, 1819, they defeated the Spanish at Boyacá (boh•yah•KAH). Two weeks later Bolívar rode victoriously into Bogotá (boh•goh•TAH), the capital of Colombia. Fearing for their lives, the local Spanish officials had already fled the city. The battle at Boyacá was a turning point in the war. The Spanish would never regain control of their colonies.

By the end of 1821, most of Colombia and Venezuela had been freed from Spanish rule. Bolívar wasn't ready to rest. He was already thinking of his next move: liberating Ecuador. He and the other leaders of the rebellion wanted all the Spanish colonies to be free.

Taking the rebellion to Ecuador meant crossing the Andes again. Of the 3,000 rebel soldiers who started the climb, only 2,000 finished it. In the spring of 1822, the fighting began, high

in the mountains. By late May, Ecuador had also been freed. In June, Bolívar and his troops rode into the capital city of Quito (KEE•toh). During the celebration that followed, Bolívar met a young woman named Manuela Sáenz. They remained together for the rest of his life.

One important colony remained in the hands of the Spanish—Peru. Bolívar and other revolutionary leaders were concerned that Peru would be a base for the Spanish, who would try to defeat the rebellion once more. The Spanish had to be driven out of South America once and for all. So Bolívar led an army into Peru.

In August 1824, Bolívar and his 9,000 soldiers defeated the Spanish army at Junín (hoo•NEEN), southeast of Lima (LEE•mah). Four months later the last important battle in the colonies' fight for freedom took place at Ayacucho (eye•uh•KOO•choh). The rebels again defeated the Spanish troops. Peru was free.

A year later Upper Peru (now Bolivia) also claimed its independence and named itself after Bolívar. Members of George Washington's family sent Bolívar a gold medal that had once belonged to the U.S. President. The family praised Bolívar as "the second Washington of the New World."

Bolívar's second-in-command, Antonio José de Sucre, led the rebel troops against the Spanish Army at the Battle of Ayacucho.

Some of Bolívar's dreams had come true. The Spanish colonies of South America had become independent. Bolívar had won many battles and had experienced great glory. By 1826, the republics of Venezuela, Colombia, Ecuador, Peru, and Bolivia had each chosen him as their leader.

Bolívar's greater dream—a united South America—would never come true. After the revolution, the new republics began fighting among themselves. Bolívar's dream of an end to slavery also did not happen in his lifetime. The world after the rebellion did not seem better to him. He began to believe that the revolution—and his life—had been a waste.

Bolívar did have enemies. Not all the people of his country believed in his dream or in him. In 1828 he barely escaped being assassinated. His health began to fail. Discouraged by what he saw around him, he made plans to leave South America. Before he could act on his plans, he became seriously ill. His travels—and his life—ended in the village of Santa Marta, in Colombia. Bolívar spent his last days rereading *Don Quixote*. The Liberator died on December 17, 1830, in the home of a Spanish officer who had once been his enemy. Simón Bolívar was 47 years old.

After Bolívar's death, his sisters asked to have their brother's body shipped to Venezuela. It wasn't until 1842 that a ship carrying his remains left Santa Marta with a fleet sailing for Caracas. On December 17, 1842, the twelfth anniversary of Bolívar's death, a grand funeral procession moved through the streets of Caracas. Crowds of mourners at last welcomed home their great liberator. Members of Bolívar's family and two elderly women—his beloved caretakers Hipólita and Matea—were among them.

For 20 years Simón Bolívar had fought hard for independence and freedom. He played a key role in liberating Bolivia, Colombia, Ecuador, Peru, and Venezuela from Spanish rule. Today Bolívar is honored and celebrated throughout much of South America. His birthday is a national holiday in Bolivia and in Venezuela. He may not have achieved all of his dreams, but he did more than any could expect of one person. His dream of extending democracy and freedom is still alive today.

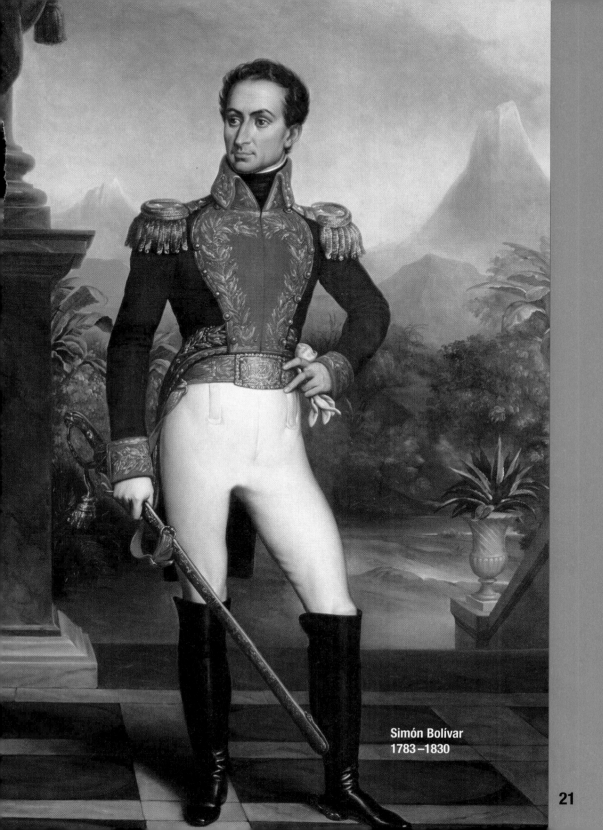

Simón Bolívar
1783–1830

TFK SPOTLIGHT

- Born July 24, 1783 in Caracas, Venezuela
- Died December 17, 1830, in Santa Marta, Colombia
- Known as El Libertador, or the Liberator, and as the George Washington of South America
- Had as family members one older brother and two older sisters
- Married from May 1802 to January 1803, to María Teresa de Toro
- Favorite book was *Don Quixote*, by Spanish writer Miguel de Cervantes

A statue of Bolívar on the island of Saba in the Dutch West Indies shows how revered the Liberator is throughout the Western Hemisphere.

Spanish Colonies Gain Their Freedom

COUNTRY	YEAR OF INDEPENDENCE
Chile	1810
Colombia	1810
Mexico	1810
Paraguay	1811
Venezuela	1811
Argentina	1816
Peru	1821
Ecuador	1822
Bolivia	1825
Uruguay	1825

Source: *The World Fact Book*, 2001

On July 24, 2001, a child in Caracas, Venezuela, takes part in the celebration of the 218th anniversary of Simón Bolívar's birth.